LIFE LESSONS
for Mothers

by Cindy Francis

Andrews and McMeel
A Universal Press Syndicate Company
Kansas City

Library of Congress Catalog Card Number: 95-77562

ISBN: 0-8362-0822-6

Originally published in 1993 by Newport House, Inc.

First Printing, August 1995
Second Printing, February 1996
Third Printing, November 1997

To My Mother,
Donna Kress

INTRODUCTION

Years ago, when I was expecting, I had many long talks with my mother about what she had learned while raising me and my five brothers and sisters. She had done a wonderful job, while having a lot more fun than other mothers I knew. What, I wondered, were her secrets? My mother and I would talk and talk, and after she would go, I'd write down the lessons I had learned.

As a mother, I've followed these simple lessons and added my own, and I've been greatly rewarded for having them to guide and inspire me. The "terrible twos" were—for me—"terrific twos," and all the years since have been the richest of my life.

Following the publication of my first book, *Life Lessons for Women,* many of you wrote to ask me to put together another book especially for mothers. I was delighted and called the most successful and happy mothers I know to ask if they had any lessons to add. Also, I've looked through lots of books by "experts," and found that the gist of what they had to say could usually be put in a sentence or two.

I'm excited and pleased to present you now with my life lessons for mothers. I hope you'll not only read and enjoy them, but will take them to heart and *live* them. They can bring you lots of joy and love and ease. I know.

The greatest gift you have to give your children is you.

 When you talk to your child, mostly listen.

 Take care of yourself, so you can take care of others.

Change is inevitable, so welcome it.

 Always give in to the urge to hug your child.

 Setting limits is good for children. They'll complain, but what they'll feel is *relief*.

You'll never be an "Absolutely Perfect Mother." Be a "Good Enough Mother."

 If things don't work out, it's okay to cry— but also *learn*.

 Teach your children they're unique. That way, they won't feel pressure to be like everybody else.

Ask your child what she most likes to do with you. Do that more often.

 Say "I'm sorry" when you're wrong.

 Your child will do as you do, not as you say. So set a good example.

Catch your child doing things *right*.

 Be loving, even when you don't feel loving.

 Forgive yourself for the mistakes you have made.

Encourage your child every chance you get.

 Be flexible with rules.

 Recognize and accept your child's feelings.

Look for win/win solutions.

 Remember that when you tell your children to act their age, they probably already are.

 Sometime each day, give your child your undivided attention.

Ask for your child's opinion more often.

 If you feel overwhelmed, just start doing one thing at a time.

 Tell your children, "I love you just the way you are."

Take time out every day
to have fun.

Give your children opportunities to make *real* contributions to the family.

 Go to the park. *Everybody* plays!

 Don't compare your children to others. Value them each for their own gifts.

Life Lessons you can learn from your children:

- Play more.

- Be curious.

- Get all wrapped up in what you're doing.

- Even the littlest things can bring you pleasure.

Treat your children the way you wish you had been treated when you were a youngster.

 Show your respect by introducing your child by name to everyone who comes over.

Be your child's biggest fan.

Exercise together.

 When your child is angry, say out loud,
"I think you need a big hug"—and then
give it!

 Having your house look like *House Beautiful*
isn't a good use of time. Settle for *House
Pretty Clean.*

Get up early and watch the sunrise together.

 Tell your child, "My life is so much better because you are here."

 Build an extended family, whether it's made up of relatives or friends.

Plant a tree together.

 When there's conflict, focus on the role *you* play.

 To belong is your children's underlying goal—even when they're misbehaving. Give them constructive ways to belong.

Go to a parade.

 Spend time together in the library.

 Ask questions that begin with "How," "Why,"
and "Tell me about." These encourage
children to speak up.

Build your children's self-esteem by letting them solve most of their own problems.

 Have a special time each week for you and your child to do something together. With a teenager, ask for this time because you need it.

Go to a pond and skip stones.

 Children will believe what you say. So be sure what you say builds them up.

 Do what *you* feel is right for your children, regardless of what "everyone else" is doing.

Teach that what other kids say about them is just *opinion*, not the *truth*.

 If you work, don't feel guilty. Every single study ever done shows children of working mothers do just as well as other children.

Be grateful for your family—
problems and all.

Have more family picnics.

 Go bird-watching together.

 Nothing happens by itself. You have to *work* at having a good family life.

Let your children have their own books.

 Give up comparing your family with the *Brady Bunch/Father Knows Best* images you grew up with. Those were TV fantasies; your family is real.

Bake cookies together from scratch.

 Take time to be apart from your children.
It will give you all a chance to grow.

 Given a little training and a little practice,
most children can far exceed our
expectations.

Toast the sunset with a glass of juice.

 Children act up when they feel useless. Let them help with cooking, gardening, record keeping. And when they're older, help them find jobs.

Praise your child for sharing.

 Keep your perspective. Problems "come to pass"—not to stay.

 Meet your children's friends. Meet their parents, too, and keep in touch with them so you can compare notes.

Compliment more than
you criticize.

Teach your children good eating habits when they're young and they'll keep them all their lives.

 Have family projects like putting up a birdhouse, planting a garden, and starting a family photo album.

Encouragements kids would benefit from hearing more often:

- "Thanks! You really made a difference."

- "I couldn't have done it better myself."

- "I enjoyed working on that with you."

- "You've improved!"

- "I have faith in you."

Even if your child isn't good at listening to you, she will certainly be good at imitating you.

 Give your children problems like, "How can we cut our electricity bill?" Let them research answers and help with solutions.

Have your children learn first aid.

 Let your children know they can always express themselves freely to you about everything.

 Take a nature hike together.

Have your own outside interests. Don't live through your children.

 Teach your children your family's history, the struggles and successes that led to all of you being where you are.

Talk about values if you expect your child to have values.

 Most things that *can* go wrong, don't.

 When things *do* go wrong, keep your perspective in describing them. Most aren't "terrible," just unfortunate.

*K*eep your promises.

Have everybody help recycle newspapers.

 Help your child become an expert at *something*, whether it's playing the flute, ballet, karate, or baseball cards.

 You'll never get everyone's approval of everything you do as a mother. So don't bother trying.

Tell your children how proud you are of them.

 Let your children know that if there's trouble, you'll always be there.

 Invite to your home positive people who feel good about themselves.

Let your children "overhear" you praising them.

 Watch for the evening star together. Make a wish.

 Make sure your child understands new rules. Do this by asking them to tell you the rule in their own words.

Have Polynesian night, with everyone dressed like natives.

 Hear your children out, even if you think your answer will be no.

 Make it clear your love doesn't depend on their performance.

Talk about the life lessons to be learned from other people's mistakes.

 Everyone—not just *you*—can help out around the house.

 Read *Children, The Challenge* to learn better ways to raise responsible children.

Make it clear *you* like compliments too. When you do a good job, say, "Okay, I'm open for compliments!"

 It's easy for mothers to become isolated. Spend time with friends. And if you don't have them, *make* them.

When you need help,
ask for it.

Have a family movie night, complete with pizza and popcorn.

 Be firm where safety is concerned.

 If your child has problems with schoolwork, get help right away, before he gets really behind.

Put on an old Chubby Checker record and twist with your child.

 To relate better, sit or kneel down on your child's level.

 If your child has an overcrowded schedule, help him cut out something.

If your child wants to talk or play when you're busy, set a time and promise him attention then.

 Although you have a powerful connection, your child is separate and has different needs, emotions, and desires. Respect them.

Go bike riding together.

 If you've got questions about your child's behavior, ask other mothers.

 If you've got serious questions, see a pediatrician or counselor. Ask for help for both your child *and you*.

Work on problems while they're small.

Share with your child your own life lessons.

 Read *The Giving Tree* together.

 Balance is the key. Balance work with play; balance time with the children with time alone.

When you listen, focus on what your child is *feeling*.

 Be sure your child gets familiar with computers.

 You are not responsible for everything going well for everyone all the time.

Ask your children questions about things *they* are interested in.

 For one day, count how many times you criticize—and praise—your children. Work at criticizing less and praising more.

Talk problems out.

 When you're working around the house, explain what you're doing and ask for help.

 Plan family activities, so watching TV isn't the only thing to do.

Show your children you're
on their side.

Pause and take stock of what *really* matters to you. Put your time and energy *there*.

 Quality time is important, but sometimes so is the quantity of time.

Visualize success for yourself and your children.

 Give your children some privacy.

 Tell your child what *to* do instead of what *not* to do.

Take a warm bubble bath after the kids are in bed.

 As your children grow older, the way you treat them needs to keep pace. Much teenage rebellion comes from treating them like they're ten when they're fifteen.

Have everyone in the family name three things every other person does well.

 Read *How to Get Control of Your Time and Your Life* to get organized.

 Give your full attention when you talk. Don't read or watch TV.

Teach your children there are better ways to solve problems than whining and hitting.

 Instead of ordering your kids to put on sweaters and jackets, let them carry them; they'll put them on if they feel cold.

*Tell your children how special
they are to you.*

Make having fun a priority!

 To produce a happy child, be a happy parent.

 Every weekend, explore together someplace new in your area.

Get involved in your child's education by working positively with the school.

 Read *Calvin and Hobbes* together. Ask why the characters act the way they do.

Blow up a balloon and play volleyball with it.

 Important lesson: *life isn't fair.*

 Tell your children "I love you," each morning before they leave home.

You can teach your children how to clean their rooms, but don't expect too much.

 Punish your children by giving "time-outs" and by withdrawing privileges.

It takes two to make an argument.
Don't be one of them.

 Get the *Consumer Reports Buying Guide*,
and when you're going shopping, let your
child pick out the best buy.

Nurture your child—
not just with food,
but with kind words as well.

Get together with other mothers and swap stories.

 Start a journal to keep track of what you've learned and the successes you've had.

 Get a book on parenting and look up what to expect at your child's age.

Have lighthearted "punishments":

- Whoever has her elbows on the table must sing a song.

- Swear words = 10 cents.

- Saying something negative about another family member = 25 cents.

Enjoy the gifts life is presenting you at this moment.

 Never criticize in front of others.

 When you're upset, be careful not to say things you might regret.

Take lots of pictures.

 Sometime, when your children expect punishment, give them a big hug instead.

 For a laugh, read together the *George and Martha* books, the *Cut-Ups* books, and anything else by James Marshall.

Show your love by being kind.

 Growth comes with frustration. Be a source of support.

 Once you have criticized your child's actions, don't bring it up again.

Tell your child often
"I love you, no matter what."

Set reasonable limits.

 At bedtime, establish a routine that winds things down and gets your child ready for sleep.

 Have fruits and vegetables—instead of candy—for your kids to snack on.

Think how you'd feel
in your child's place.

Have a special dinner in honor of your children.

 Share memories of when you were your child's age.

 When your children get discouraged, remind them of all the things they couldn't do not long ago—and now can.

At night, sit outside on a blanket and look at the stars.

 Hold family meetings to clear up gripes.

 Set up a tent in the living room and have dinner in it.

Treat all your children equally.

 Have your kids take music lessons, but let them quit if they don't like it.

 Rituals, like having dinner together, make children feel more secure.

Even if your child fails, praise the effort.

 How to communicate when you and your child are mad: One person talks at a time. The listener has to give back the gist of what the talker says to the talker's satisfaction before she gets her turn to speak.

Arguing Do's:

- Bring up one problem at a time.
- Focus on the problem.
- Be specific about your complaints.
- Compromise if possible.

Arguing Don'ts:

- No yelling or swearing.

- No name calling.

- No questioning motives.

- No bringing up the past.

*Praise—not just success—
but also improvement.*

Lie on the floor and read the encyclopedia together.

 Your children provide you with a second chance to do the things you loved as a youngster. Take that chance.

Cook a meal together, with everybody in charge of one dish.

 If you're too busy to have fun with your children, you're too busy.

 When you're driving, hand your child a map and ask her to direct you to your destination.

Compliment your children often, and you'll give them a reputation to live up to!

 Let your children progress at their own speed.

If the discipline you're using isn't working, do something different.

 The behavior may be bad, but never the child.

 If you expect your children to be "perfect," you will always be disappointed.

See who can make the funniest face.

 Teach that failure is never final unless you give up.

 Once a month, spend a whole day doing whatever your child wants to do.

Be happy as your children need you less and less. That's how it's *supposed* to be.

 Teach that while the easy way in the *short* run is to be lazy and goof off in school, that often turns out to be the hard way in the *long* run.

Pause and notice the beauty
around you.

Three steps to take when children misbehave:

1. Briefly describe the behavior.

2. Tell how you feel about it.

3. Affirm that you know the child can do better.

Instead of coaxing your children out of bed every morning, buy them alarm clocks. If they're late, let them experience the consequences.

 Stay out of your children's fights unless someone is in danger. Let them work things out themselves.

Surprise your child with little gifts.

 The best way to get your children to listen to you is to listen to them.

 Let family privileges coincide with responsibilities.

Never say your child is "shy." Instead, explain, "She doesn't want to talk right now."

 If your child acts shy, practice with her in front of a mirror smiling, making eye contact, and keeping her legs and arms uncrossed.

Tell your children stories in which *they* are the heroes.

 When your kids grow up, they won't remember whether the house was perfectly neat and clean. But they will remember whether or not you spent time with them.

*B*etter to be a model
than a critic.

When you get angry, remember it's the result of *your* thinking, not what your child is doing.

 Teach that no one is perfect—not you, not them, not anyone. And nothing is perfect. But it's possible to be happy in an imperfect world.

Seek first to understand, then to be understood.

 When your child tells you problems, show you really understand by repeating the essence of what you heard and asking if you're right.

*When you're excited,
let it show!*

Have talks at bedtime. Your child will talk more in order to stay up later.

 With teenagers, have talktime while driving and while eating pizza.

Fly a kite together.

 Send your children off in the morning with a hug.

 A positive word or smile every day can propel your child to success.

Replenish yourself by taking time to be alone.

Help a charity drive together.

 The only person you can control is yourself.

 Build trust by going on a "blind hike," in which you take turns closing your eyes and being led around the neighborhood.

Encourage your child to think BIG!

 Teach your children the *immediate* bad consequences of smoking—it makes you cough and your breath and clothes smell bad. Children seldom think long-term.

Teach also the *immediate* bad consequences of drinking—it makes it hard for you to think and learn and play. It makes you say and do stupid things you may regret later. And it often makes you have bad accidents.

 Have everyone tape a message to send to someone far away.

Don't do for children what they can do for themselves.

 When your children outgrow clothes, give them to the poor.

 For one day, keep track of all the sugar your child eats. Put that amount in a bottle and show it to her.

Report cards are your *child's*—not *yours.*

 Let your children see that you have short-comings and suffer setbacks. This will help them be more realistic about themselves.

Nurture yourself too.

Go to garage sales together.

 Help your child plan short-term goals
(like going camping) and long-term goals
(like going to college).

 Let your child have input into solutions
for problems, especially those which
concern her.

If you can afford it, get help with your housework.

 Try to have a sit-down family meal at least three times a week. Turn off all distractions like the TV and stereo.

 When your child takes a wrong turn, gently help her get back on track.

Keep instructions simple.

 Play with your child every day.

 Plan your child's parties around activities like swimming and bowling.

Be consistent.

Attend your child's school activities.

 Mark off your children's height on a closet wall. Watch them grow!

 You can't *assume* your kids understand their homework. Look it over to see if they need help.

Visualize the outcomes you want.

 Put a surprise love note under everybody's plate at dinner.

 When you're angry, take five minutes to cool off.

Kids sometimes have to make their own mistakes before they learn from them.

 At bedtime, get the conversation going by asking, "What's the best thing that happened to you today? The worst?"

Use the past tense when criticizing. For example, say "you forgot" rather than "you always forget."

 Let your child take responsibility for her actions—and for coping with what follows.

Read your children stories about successful people.

 Be specific with praise. It will mean more.

 Make a list of everything you have to do each day. Do the most important first.

Shower your kids with kindness!

 Be honest (they'll know if you're not, anyway).

 Have "Family Night" once a week. Everybody does something fun together.

*Follow the rules yourself
that you set for your child.*

Have a family Ping-Pong contest!

 Read *The Value of Honesty* with your child.

 If you work, take your child with you so she'll understand what it is you do.

Give gifts that encourage fitness, such as skates and bikes.

 Substitute low-fat frozen yogurt for ice cream, graham crackers for chocolate chip cookies, popcorn for potato chips.

Always be on the lookout for something positive to say.